Naively Young Heart

A Collection of Love Poems

Nani S.

BookLeaf Publishing

India | USA | UK

21. Final Thought

Life gets flexed.
Not broken apart.
Any ending.
Is simply a new start.
Easy tasks, do not last.
Difficult climbs, earn vision to the blind.
Impulsive thoughts, generate dangerous plots.
Rationalizing time, navigates to the sublime.
Wisdom is listening more, speaking less.
Vocalize to be heard, know what topics to address.
Move in the shadows.
Radiate light.
Never bow to a knee.
Stand firmly on feet.
Everyone dies.
Not everyone lives.

Made with ❤ on the BookLeaf Publishing Platform
www.bookleafpub.in
www.bookleafpub.com

Dedication

For those who have loved and lost, for those still searching, and for those who have found a home in another's heart. This book is for you.

Preface

In the quiet moments of life, when the world slows and thoughts wander, the heart often finds its voice. "Naively Young Heart: A Collection of Love Poems" is the echo of such moments—a tender chronicle of a young woman navigating the intricate landscapes of love. It is a journey through the tenderness of first blush, the ache of longing, the joy of connection, and the quiet reflections that love inspires.

Each poem is a glimpse into the intimate world of a soul awakening to the beauty and complexity of affection. Here, love is not merely an emotion but a transformative experience, shaping and reshaping the contours of the self. It is a force that elevates and humbles, ignites passion, and stirs contemplation.

Acknowledgements

Firstly, to the readers—thank you for opening your hearts to these poems. It is my deepest hope that you find echoes of your own experiences in these pages, and that the words bring you comfort, joy, and a sense of connection. To the loves that inspired these verses—both those that stayed and those that did not—I am grateful. You have taught me the many shades of love and helped me understand the depths of my own heart.

1. Forever Yours

Can I tell you something?
Would've never thought about it
I think I'm falling for you
So badly, don't know what to do
What do you say now
How about we tie the knot?
I wanna be the one that's down
Don't ever wanna see you frown.
Someone like you
I don't wanna lose
Gotta make this right
I wanna be with you day and night.
Since we're apart
I know this is hard
We'll be together one day.
But for now just let me say
I'm your protector
You are my target to save
I wouldn't put you in harm
Never would cause it

And now I want to be with you.
Cherish us, cherish the good times
And the bad times
No matter what we're one
Believe in us, we'll conquer the world
Just know I'm forever yours.

2. Love is My Challenge

Nights, when I lay in bed
Things run through my mind
The thoughts of fear and trouble
Risks and consequences soon to arise
Within my heart, within my soul, I ask myself
"Why do I feel so empty?" "What taunts me to think this
way?" "How am I able to breathe?"
When I look into the dark sky, I want to see the stars
The stars at night calm me, fill me with the everlasting
tranquility
Inspires me to want to travel through the galaxies,
Far and wide for however long it shall take me
To feel free, but not alone.
To feel loved, to feel at home
I want to love, but there is no love
Why is there no love? Where is the love?
It's there, but I don't see it
For me, I don't want to see it
The last time I loved, it broke me
To the point where I couldn't eat for days

Just rotting my pain away
Blaming myself for the cause,
When really they were the cause of it all.
It made me not trust, it made me not see
It made me close doors, chances to what things could've
possibly been
Never wanted children, never wanted marriage,
But now contemplating on life, starting to have second
thoughts.
Now as I feel safe, do I really feel safe?
I want to feel safe, but I hate feeling this way.
When he's not there, I miss being with him
It's like he belongs here, but cannot be here
I understand it's the same for me
But I feel afraid, I feel afraid to love again
I'm afraid of getting hurt again
There are nights when I want to be held
There are days when I want to be held
The way he holds me, is the vibe that I desire.
This feeling, is a good feeling
So why do I contemplate on this connection?
That's why I do my thinking at night.
At nights, when I lay in my bed
Things run through my mind
The thoughts of fear and trouble
Risks and consequences soon to arise
Love is my fear, so much responsibility

To handle, to maintain
To jump through hurdles day by day
It's a hard test to pass
Love is what I fight, but love is what I want
Love is my challenge in life.

3. Chosen

I used to think that the world was a scary place
It was cold, but big, and I felt alone
No one understood how I felt, how afraid I was
Distant from everyone that I came in contact with
Dealing with the agony and torture of isolation
Turning away from the world, laying in a hole
Thinking of death coming my way as I lay
It wasn't easy at first, but everything I ever thought
about changed one day, only one reason,
You.
It was said that an angel sent you to me
It was said that with you, I'd feel no pain,
You were patient enough to stand by me
Patient enough for me to see the world again
I was almost a fool to let you go like that,
I'm glad that you stayed around.
Where would I be without you?
How'd I feel to lose you? I'd lose my mind.
You may not know it now, but I feel as though you're
my other half.

Out of everyone in the world..I chose you
It's sad, you know? That this world can be so bad,
But with you, it's easy to see that I can find peace within
it.
You found me broken, in pieces ready to give my life
away.
You've been trying to repair me, I appreciate it,
I used to think not everyone cares, so why should I?
What's the point? Forget it all, but when you came...
That all changed.
I can see it in your eyes that you have hope for me,
You care, and you understand me.
But if I die today, or tomorrow, or whenever the time
comes...
Just know that I love you.
So changing that. Out of everyone in this world...
You chose me.
It's crazy, you know? Here we are now,
Living in this world together. But all in all,
Thank you for bearing with me. You are a miracle,
More like.....my miracle.

4. Public and Private

There's more to the story about us
We have our past
It's not left alone
Yet, there's a little flame that still flickers
Flickers on and remains the same
You may see us act a certain way in public
But there's a difference behind closed doors
See, realize the body language that we show towards
each other
It might show distance, it may show hatred
Never let the eyes deceive your mind.
There is denial, there is disagreement about what we are
You'd assume we're done for good
While we keep that in mind and just laugh it off.
We've made it this way for a reason
The fighting and arguing is for show
The way we do things is how we protect us
What you don't know is for the better
What we do is out of love, and the love that we have is
private.

5. It's Only A matter of Time

It's only a matter of time
Before you slip away from me
Before you turn your back on me
You'll let go, without hesitation or doubt
It's only a matter of time, I don't want to look forward
to.
Anger traps the soul
It feeds on pain, it triggers, it changes you
Anger is like fire, without control, it damages
What you feel, it kills me
I know that I'm guilty on my part.
Every night, I can't sleep peacefully
You're what's on my mind at night
The thought of seeing you hurt because of me
It makes me sick to my stomach knowing that I'm the
cause of it all.
I hope that you see that I never meant to hurt you
It was all in the moment, but I took it too far
I'll admit that I was wrong

There's no excuse for what I've done
Things wouldn't have to be the way they were if I hadn't
caused the problem.
It's only a matter of time
Before you want to forget me for good
Before I lose you, I don't want to lose you
The fact that I cry at night thinking that I can't fix this
Please don't go away
I'm sorry, I hope that you can forgive me
It's only a matter of time, before you let me go
It's only a matter of time, it's only a matter of time.

6. This is a Message

This is a message
A message of peace
Something that I have to address
A confession that I must share
I don't mean to hurt you
I don't mean to ignore you
We've just been apart for a while
It's what I can no longer deal with
I hope that you can forgive me
As much as I can forgive you.
Don't give up on me
Do not give up on us
You are not perfect
I'm not perfect
You're special to me
The world may not understand that
They see you as the bad person
I still see faith within you.
Please know that I'm not angry with you
Yet, I'm only disappointed in myself

I let go too quickly
I should've been more level-headed
It's not your fault
I don't want any harm casted upon you
They might think that I'm crazy
But we all do crazy things for love
I'd like to apologize for my own faults
I'm sorry on my part.
Now that you know how I feel
I'm not hurt, I do miss you
But it's hard to tell you that now
This is a message
A message of peace
To let you understand from me, to you
That I still love you.

7. Something About You

Something about you
That I can't get over
Dreams are giving me signals
Every night I go to sleep at night
You're mainly on my mind.
I know you still feel for me,
As I still feel the same for you,
But there's one thing that must be clear
We were known to have a past by many
But now, the people around us see us as toxic.
Things are different now
I remember the days we've spent together
The physical connection we've shared
From time to time, it was perfect
Being alone with you was comforting
Your touch, your eyes and body on top of mine
Our souls intertwined as one
Those were sneaky nights.
This is a promise, an oath we both shall take
What we have is behind closed doors

In public, we're distant
Alone, we'll be secret lovers
No one must ever know about us.
What we do should be kept in the closet
If you give me your time, I'll give you my time
Show me your world, and I'll show you my galaxy
I'll give you my heart, if you give me your loyalty
I'll be your candle, if you light the way
I'll be your guardian and you'll be my protector
You'll be my guide and I'll be your follower.
If we keep things silent, we'll live in bliss
If we love this way, no one can tell us otherwise
What we have is what people can't see
The fun we have is worth it
The sneaky nights are what we enjoy.

8. Still Into You

I'm so confused
Don't know what to do
Just sitting here at home
Thinking of you
What we had has ended
Never thought we'd end it
So here I am, my love and all
Has crumbled up it took the fall
I never knew
About you two
I've had enough
I'm tired of stuff
Blowing up in my face
Thought it was just a phase
But I can't seem to get over you
It's so hard
I loved you from the start
Now I can't get you out my heart
The way you walk,
the way you talk

Your eyes and smile,
made it worth the while
I'm just trying to see
what's going on with me
Guess I'm still into you
I'm still into you
Still into you.

9. Don't Get Caught Up With Love

Love ain't no person
Love ain't nobody
We all ain't perfect
But I'm gonna do me
It's full of different emotions
Sometimes it brings you rejections
Follow your dreams
Keep your head up
Live your life, you'll be fine.
Don't get caught up
Be happy
Don't you rush, it'll come in time
Don't get caught up
You've got your life ahead of you, so do you
Love is serious
You're too young to understand
A lot of things to face
You ain't ready
Don't get caught up..

10. Love's Not A Game

Messy conversations
Trials and tribulations
I've gone through with you
Love ain't what I thought
Love is not a game, it's not at all
Blissful days, stressful nights
You don't understand
You made my heart turn to ice
And now I'm hurting inside
Love ain't what I thought
Love is not a game, it's not at all
Been cheated on, mistreated oh
It's not fun at all
You make me feel like I'm not here
Sometimes I wanna die.
Messy conversations
Trials and tribulations
I've gone through..with you
Love ain't..what I thought

Love is..not a game
It's not at all.

11. No More of You

Days by days going
I knew all along
That something would tell me
You did something wrong
They told me otherwise
You weren't the one
I'm tired of playing
With you, I'm just done.
There's no trying
I'm done crying
Love is long gone
Just leave so that I can move on.
Take your stuff
I don't want anything from you
I'm over you
No apologies needed
You did enough
Time for us flew
Lies you've told, they didn't phase me
I don't want no more of you from here and out.

At nights, you'd leave me
Alone with my fears
Just laying in bed all night
Laying in tears
Then I'd sit by the the phone
Thinking of you
But then when I called you,
Her voice I heard too.
You said you loved her
You didn't want no other
All of my hurting will end today
Don't look back, just go away.
This wasn't fair
He doesn't care
As of today,
I'm no longer your bae
He'll do this to you
Girl, why can't you see too?
He's had a ball
I thought I gave my all
Don't come back to me
'Cause now that I'm free
You reap what you sew
It's fine, now I can let go.

12. Unnoticed Heartbreak

Passing by
My old flame
We used to talk
Now we don't talk at all
All my days were filled
With so much joy
Now I'm back where I began
Alone and unhappy.
There's a misunderstanding
That I can't crack
The love was all colors
But now it's all black
I can't get my feelings,
My mind through this guy
He leaves me with no care
Unnoticed, I cry.
Have you ever loved someone
Who didn't love you
They'd say they'll never let you go
But now you're pushed away

How can I leave when you made me this way
But I guess have no choice
As you walk away, I go my way in pain.
Passing by him and her
They look happy while I'm alone
How did we go from something beautiful
To something meaningless
You left me like I was just dust
A misunderstanding
That I can't crack
Was it something that I did
Something I lacked
He's not coming back
Since he'd told me goodbye
I can't take this pain so
Unnoticed, I cry.
Have you ever loved someone
Who didn't love you
They'd say they'll never let you go
But now you're pushed away
How can I leave when you made me this way
But I guess have no choice
As you walk away, I go my way in pain.
Passing by
One last time
It's hard to see, you without me
It's okay, I'll be fine

I wish you two the best
And I'll move on to see where life leads next.

13. Moving Forward

Sometimes I wanna travel through the galaxies
Just leave earth for a while and unwind
I've got a lot on my mind
There's no explaining why
I need to get away, to regain my life
I look in the mirror, see myself
Obviously that's somebody else
What have I become, this ain't alright
The pain I've endured
Had trapped me for so long
I overcame my past, now I'm on the move
No more toxicity, no more animosity
I crave for tranquility, I long for serendipity
I'm over it, I don't wanna cry no more
How he tried to lure me back
Said he's sorry and he missed me
Oh no, looks like you're out of time
My soul is at peace, God is on my side
I put myself first before anyone else
I'm doing my own thing

Working hard, I'm on grind mode
Know that you are option
Don't need you, don't have to have you
With or without you, I am gonna shine
I'm gonna see the world
One day I'll accomplish my goal
You'll see, people are gonna know my name
I was once a wilted flower
Had to pick up my petals, and recover alone
Now I'm blooming, benefitting for my soul
I'll be productive, not destructive
Gotta do what I gotta do for my own
Maybe not today, maybe not tomorrow
But someday you'll understand,
Losing me will be your downfall
You'll do you and I'll do me
Somebody will see the star in me
Believe.

14. Where Were You?

Where were you when I needed you
You were once kind and caring
But now, you are a monster
Now, you never pay attention.
To me, I thought you would be there
But you wouldn't even talk to me
So I thought that I could give you another chance
And you took advantage of my spirit.
When I wanted to go to the dance with you
All you did was laugh in my face
At night, I would toss and turn in my bed
I was full of humiliation, especially while my friend was
there.
Now that I forgot about you
I was glad to move on
And when I saw you and you realized that you needed
me back
I couldn't because now, I was with him.
He's not a cold-hearted person like you
He makes me laugh, you made me cry

He gives me hugs and you pushed me away
He brightens my day while you tried to darken it.
I wonder about you, your soul is nowhere to be found
But I just want to thank you
Because without you in my life
I never would've met him.
As I look back, I've realized something
You almost ruined my inner self
But since he brought my confidence back
I despise you, and I love him.

15. What Will Happen to You and I?

If we never see each other again
What will happen to you and I,
If our bond of love is broken
Then our relationship will die.
You complete my living soul
I love everything about you,
You always keep me company
Without you, I don't know what I'll do.
I don't care what my parents say
What I'm saying is true,
I don't care what people say
All I care about is you.
I remember the first time we met
We didn't like one another,
Now here we are, both together
Both of us fell in love with each other.
If we never see each other again
What will you do,

If you go, I want you to know
I'll always love you.

16. What Does Love Mean?

What does love mean to you
How do you describe it,
How does it feel
What does love say to you?
You were my sweetheart
I was able to trust you,
Yet you looked into my face and deceived me
You don't know what love is.
You told me that you loved me
But now I don't believe it,
I can't stand the fact that I was a fool
And I was actually falling for you.
Why would you do this
Why would you treat me this way,
There was no need for that
There's no love, no trust.
How will I trust you now I believed in you,
Yet you went and stabbed me in the heart
Now, your kisses and your touch won't phase me.
Love is special

Two souls connected as one, It joins the bond of
friendship
It's not just about romance.
Love is caring
When one understands the other,
Through communication and honesty
Both must pour out from the heart good and bad.
Love is beautiful
More than what is thought on the outside,
On the inside it's spiritual
More than about physical and mental love.
What you don't know about it
You lacked the true meaning,
As I will miss the kisses and hugs
We must move on.
People understand the importance
Love is irreplaceable,
Don't take one another for granted
Remember, love is like a flower.

17. I Have A Feeling About You

I have a feeling about you
I don't know what that feeling is,
Everytime when I see you, it's weird
You give me this strange trigger in my mind
What do I feel?
My stomach gives me butterflies
My heart is giving me a sign,
You did something to make me feel this way
You are the reason I'm feeling unusual
What do I feel?
Your looks put me in a trance
The way you walk and talk move me,
I've never felt this way before
There's something about you that makes me feel this
way
What do I feel?
I want to deny it, but I most certainly can't
Now I blush when I see you,
You make me laugh and open up to me

Everything is now coming together
What do I feel?
I have a feeling about you
A very positive feeling I have,
The way you light up a room amazes me
I think I have a crush on you
I now know what I feel.

18. I See You

I see you as an angel
You came in and saved me from my hell,
You bought light into my soul again
You took my breathe and put me in nirvana.
I see you as a superhero
You flew in and showed me a new world,
You defended and protected me from harms way
You are there when I need you.
I see you as you
Different from the others in this world,
You are the most unique and special person to me
You are the key to my heart.
I see you as a dream
A dream that is something I never wanna leave,
Something that will make me feel elated when I'm upset
You brighten me up and take my nightmares away.
I see you as mine
You make me feel important,
The person that enlightens my days is the one that is on
my mind everyday

You are my completion.
I see you as an individual
You deeply express how you feel in the most
mesmerizing way,
I love everything about you
I hope you do too.

19. The Evil of Lust

Why did you make me feel this way
You just love sitting back and watch me being tortured,
I'm stuck in this situation because of you
You are the opposite of what love is.
It's not easy being this way
This thing loves wanting to have you suffer,
It wants you trapped
It's the temptation that'll get you.
The looks, the touches, the feelings
Wanting more of what they can give you,
The desire of what you have for them
There is at some point a shortage to this.
Now it's just you, facing that person
Oh, how you felt before vanished,
You're now stuck in this trial, trying to get through the
day
The night also, but you still can't get over them.
You say that you love them, but do they really love you
too?
Do both of you still talk the way you used to,

Do you both feel the same way about each other
Let that sit in your head for a second.
Welcome to the game
You just stepped into weeks of torture,
It clouds your mind temporarily
Only thing that'll get rid of this is with the thought of
someone else.
You may still feel some way about them
But it's over for the two of you,
It was just an old flame that died eventually
The agony of it all is caused by the evil of lust.

20. What is Life?

What is life if you can't live it?
What is love if your emotions get played with?
What is hope if you stop believing in faith?
Keep your head up and move on...
It's life, stuff happens.

21. My Confession to You

I don't know what to say.
I don't know how to feel,
But there is something about you
That I can't resist.
You are more than a friend to me.
Love is more than what I'm feeling for you.
You are the one
That can take me away from pain.
You are the one
That can brighten my day.
You're not like the others that have hurt me.
The way we connect to each other
Is a dream for me.
I would admit to you if I had the chance,
But I crave only for you.
Your looks, I find intriguing.
There's no way in life
That I will never see a face like yours.
You're eyes are beautiful,
I am hypnotized every time I look into them.

As we engage
In looking into each other's eyes,
We both have this shimmer,
Like millions of stars in the moonlight.
Your body calls out to me.
I want you to step into my world,
My temple, explore me a little.
Your lips put me in a trance.
I would want to keep kissing you
Throughout the whole night
Without a pause,
Just to feel your smooth lips
Touch against mine.
It's as if I'm attracted to you,
But you aren't a magnet.
You may not see it now
But rest assure you,
That I am the girl
That has that temptation
For you and only you.
I want you to be mine
So that we can paint the town
And let the world know that we're one.
I want you to be mine
So that we can create
Beautiful music together.
We may not be saying much now,

But behind closed doors,
I still have this aching,
Burning feeling
In my soul for you.
I just wanna put that flame out
By getting close to you.
You make me feel elated
Every time I get to be with you.
I hope that one day, you'll see
That I'm madly into you.